Christmas
Memory Book

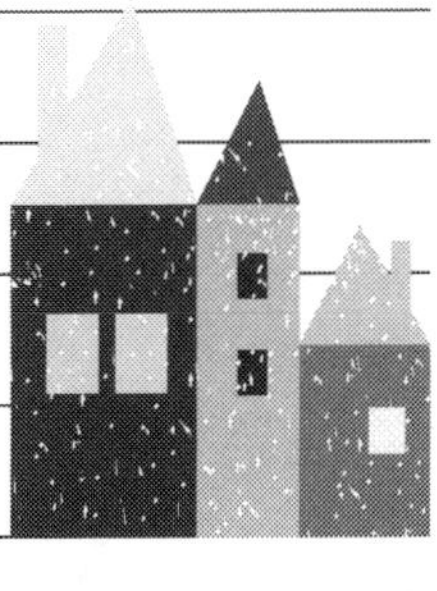

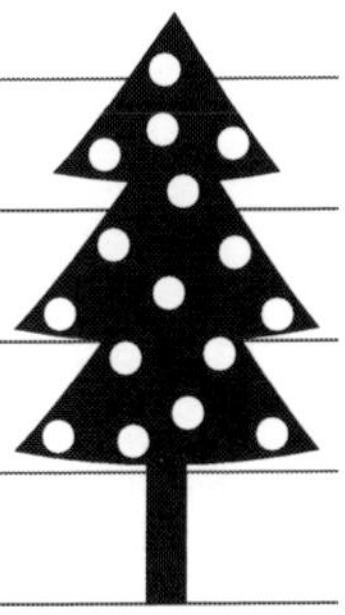

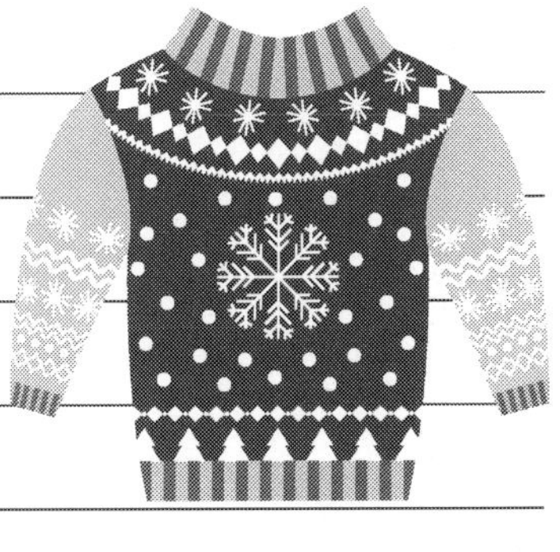

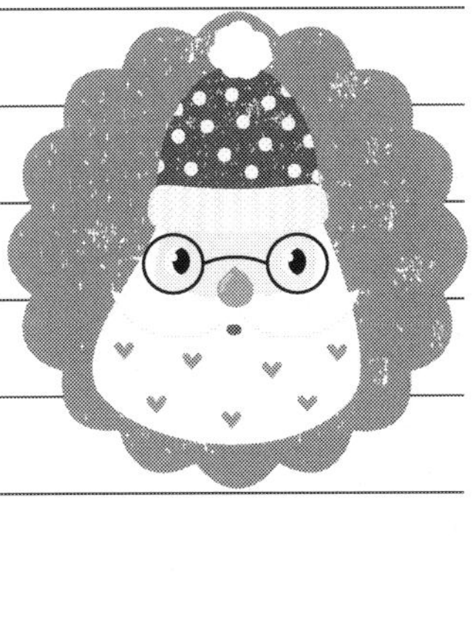

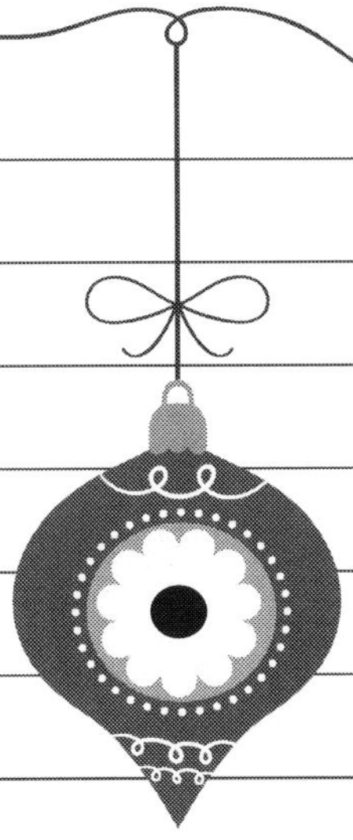

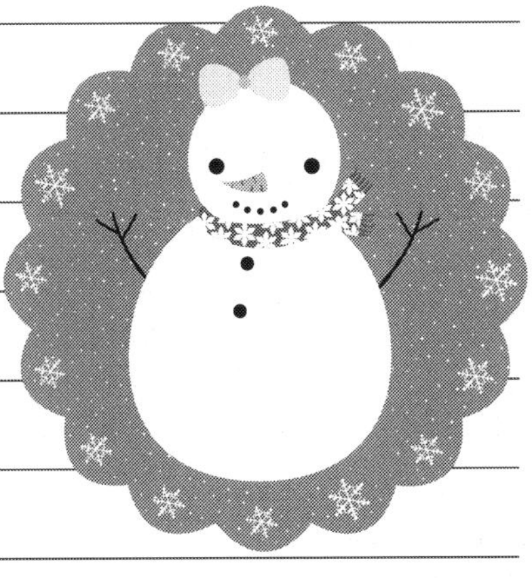

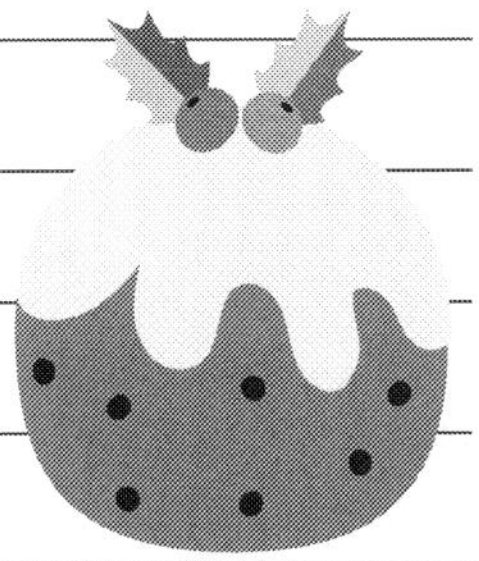

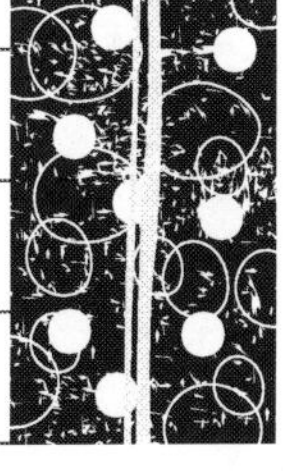

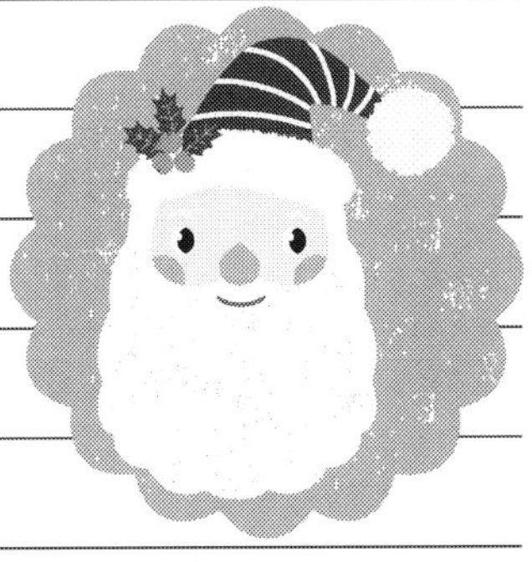

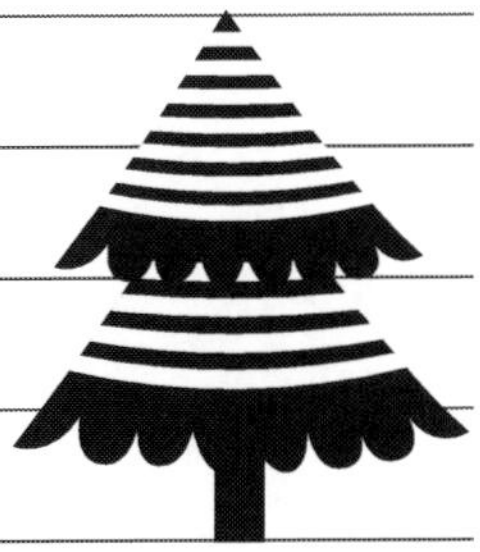

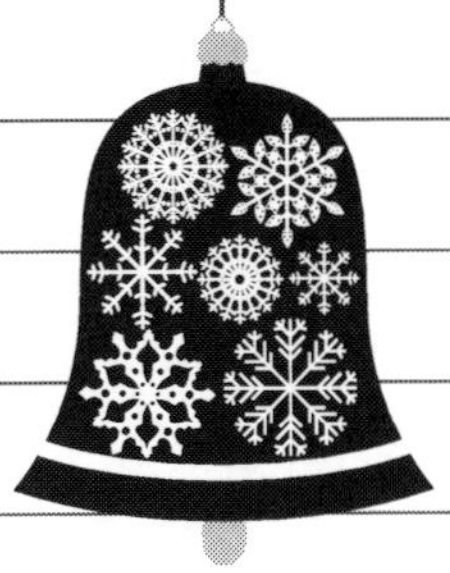

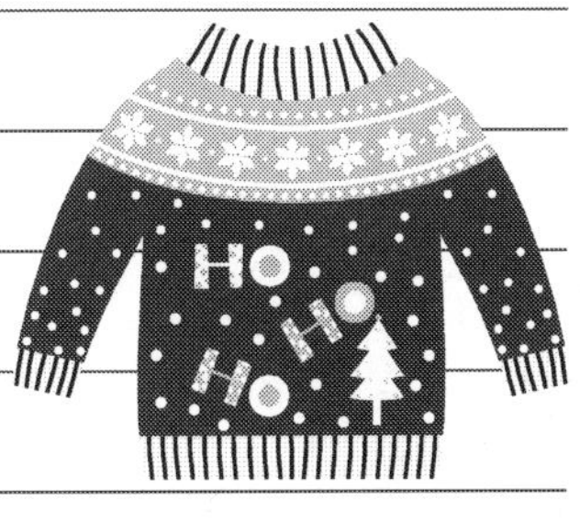
HO
HO
HO

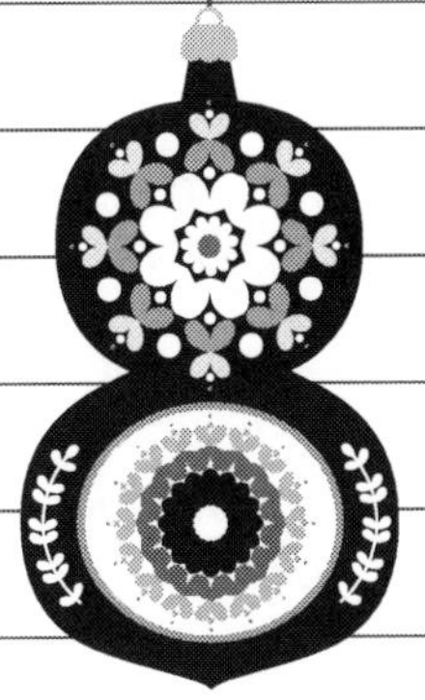

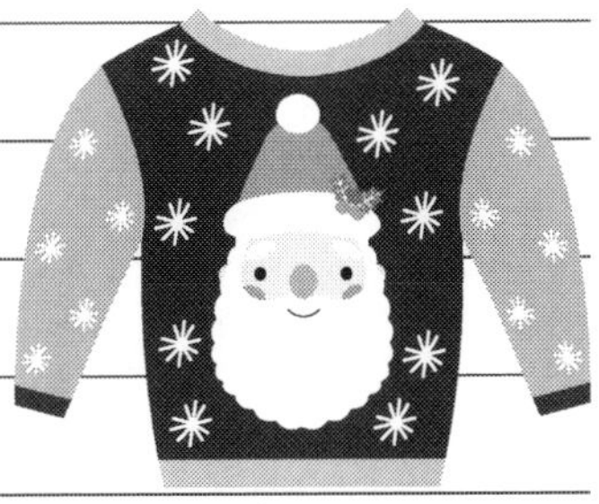

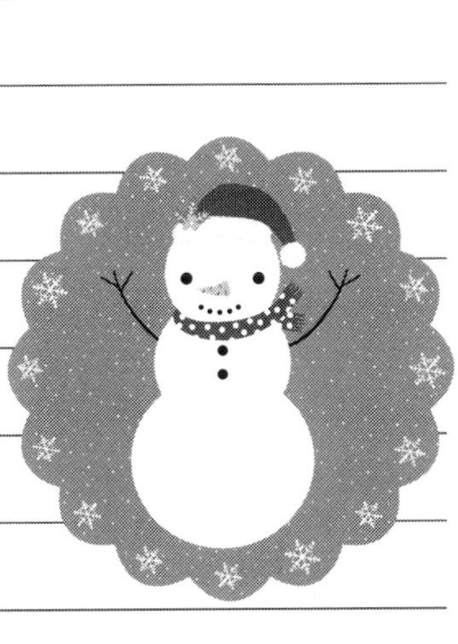

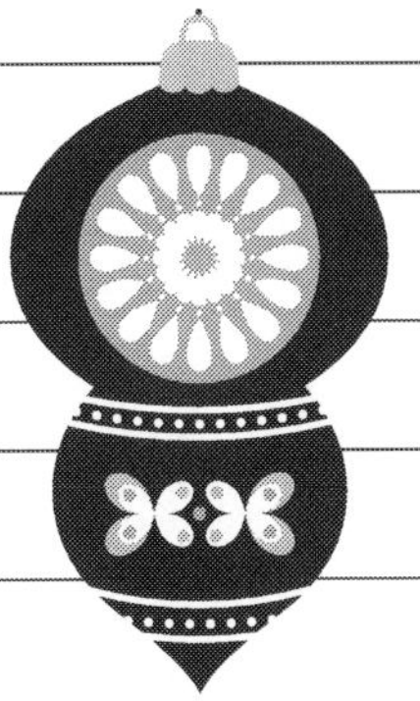

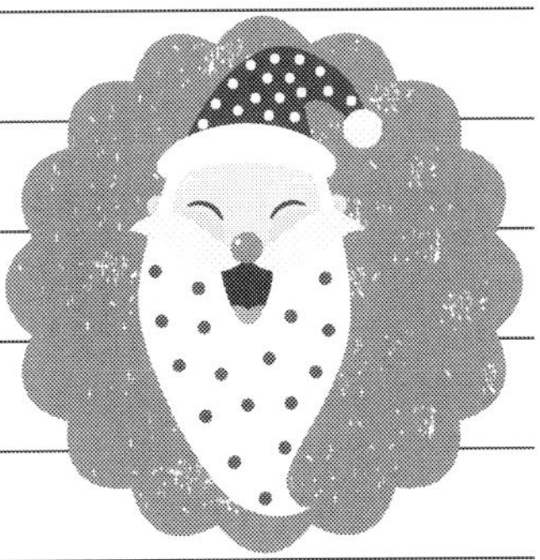

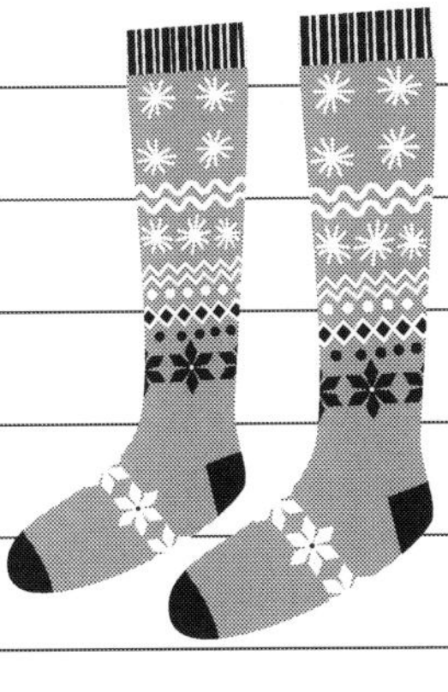

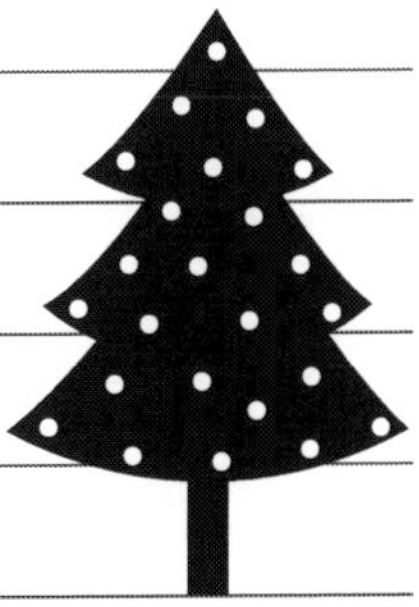

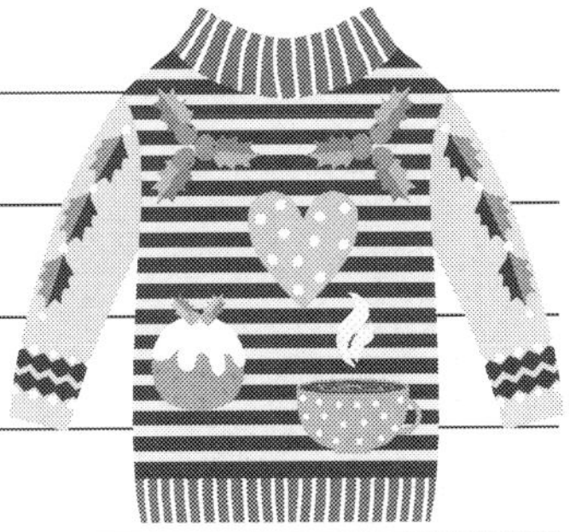

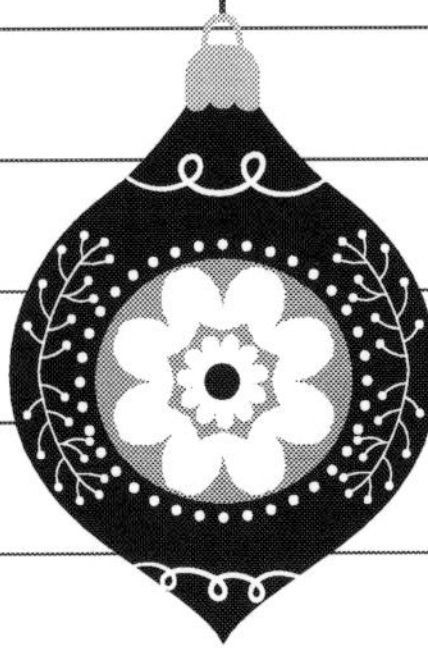

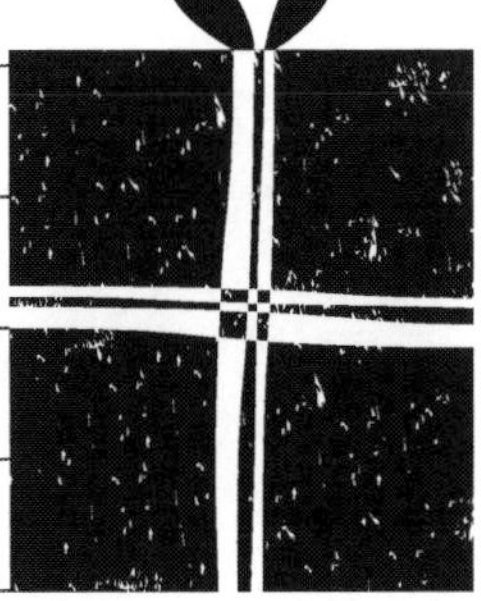

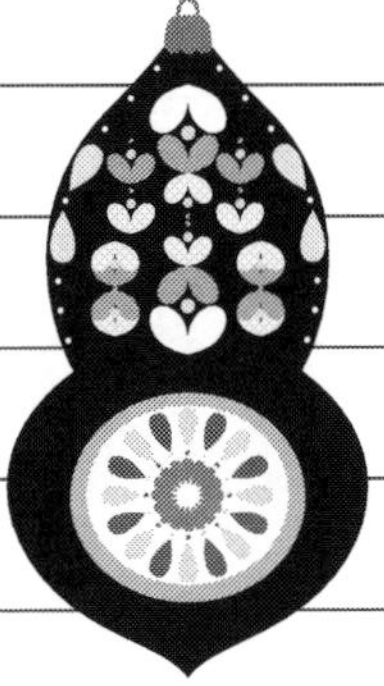

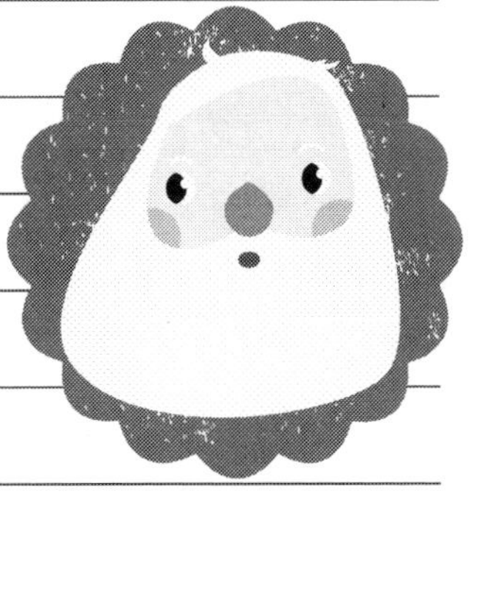

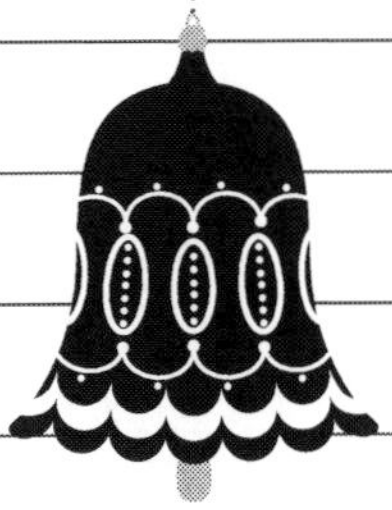

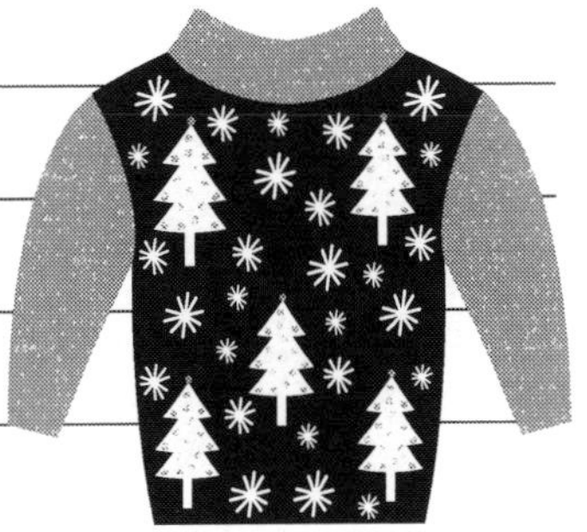

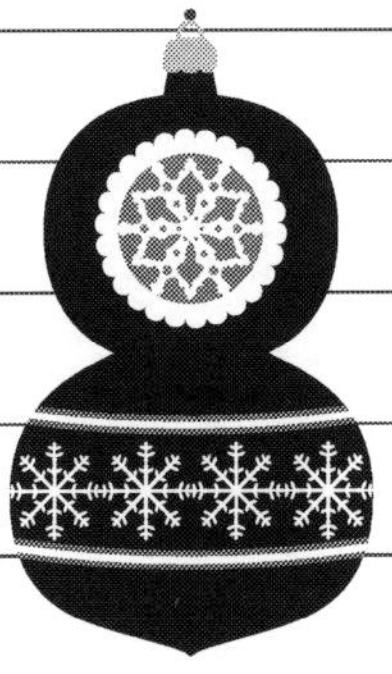

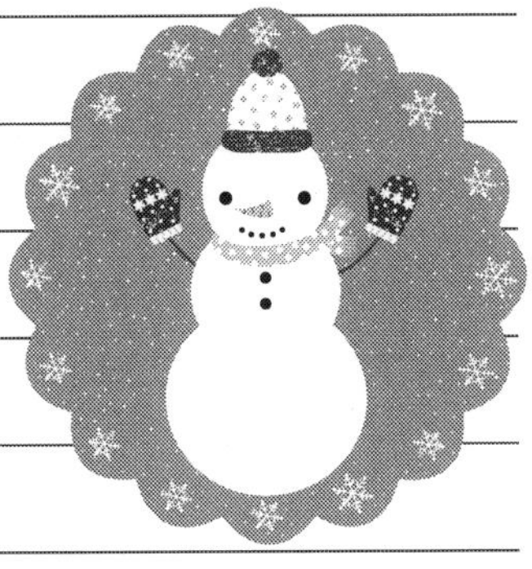

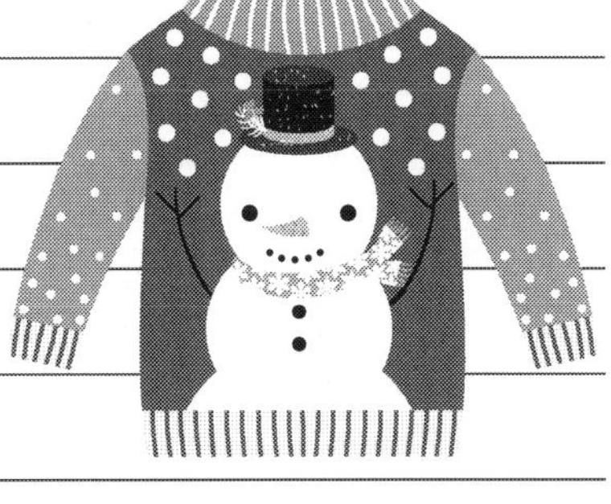

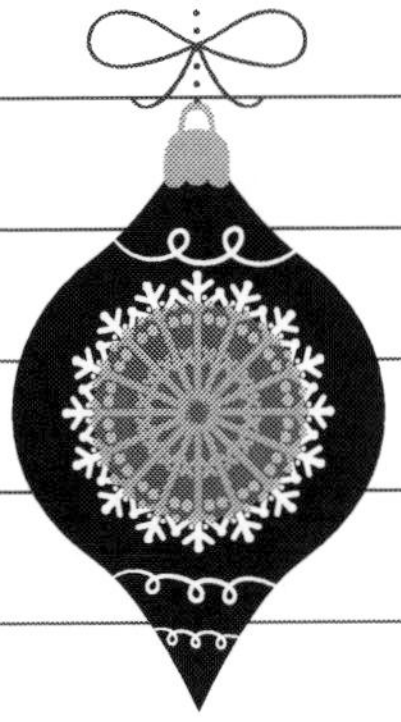

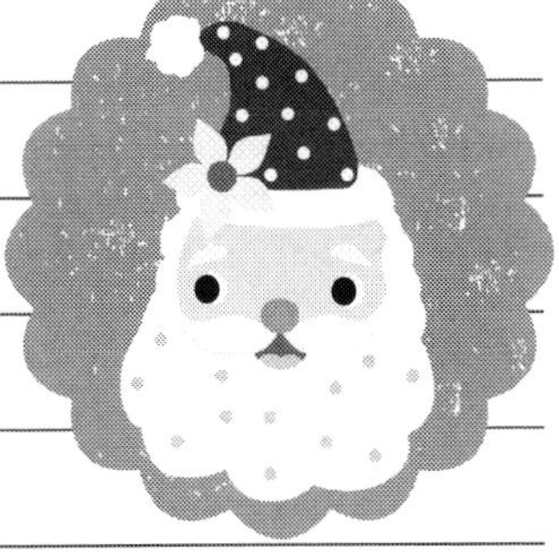

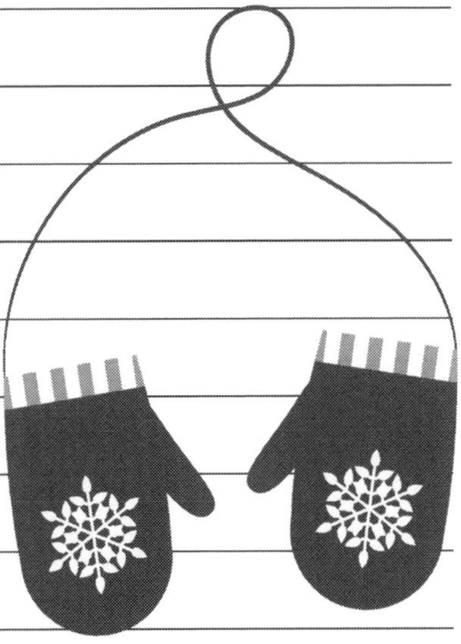

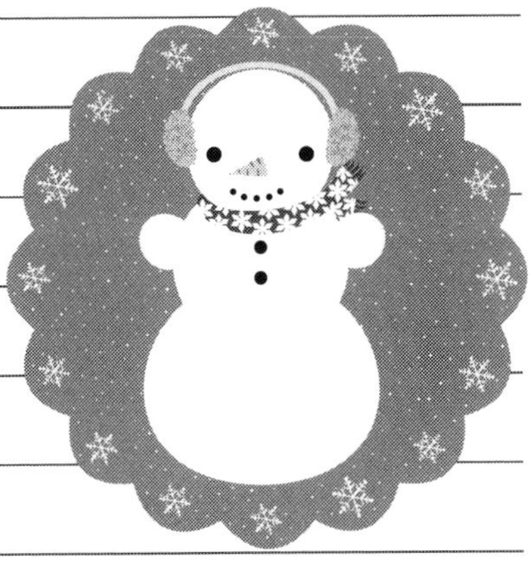

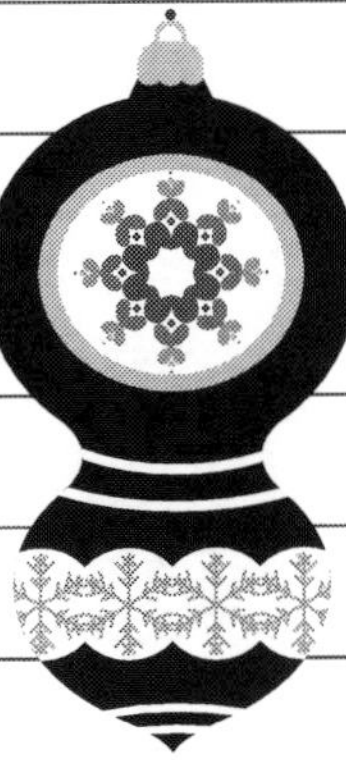

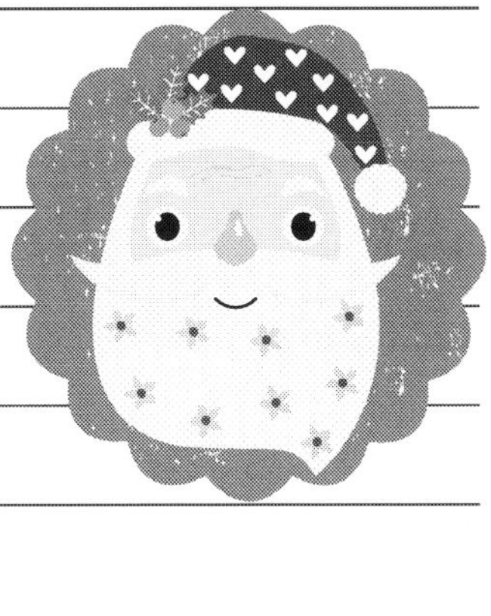

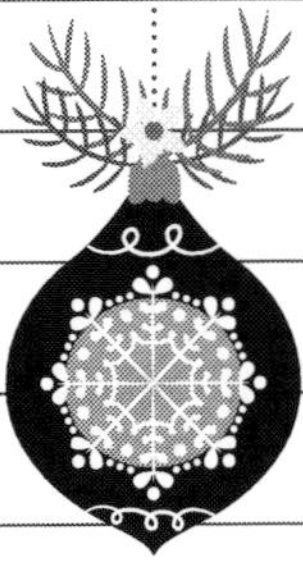

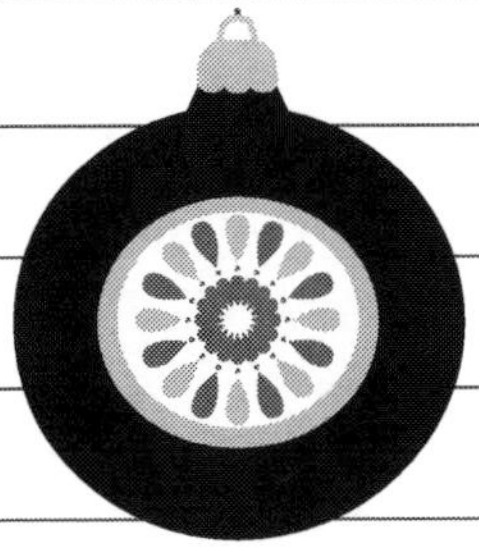

Made in the
USA
Columbia, SC

78723878R00057